MY FIRST BOOK
SPAIN

ALL ABOUT SPAIN FOR KIDS

GLOBED
CHILDREN BOOKS

Copyright 2023 by Globed Children Books

All rights reserved. No part of this book may be reproduced or distributed in any form without prior written permission from the author, with the exception of non-commercial uses permitted by copyright law.

Limited of Liability/Disclaimer of Warranty: The publisher and author make no representations or liabilities with respect to the accuracy and completeness of the contents of this work and specifically disclaim all warranties including without limitations warranties of fitness of particular purpose. No warranty may be created or extended by sales or promotional materials. This work is sold with the understanding that the publisher and author is not engaging in rendering medical, legal or any other professional advice or service. Further, readers should be aware that websites listed in this work may have changed or disappeared between when this work was written and when it is read.

Interior and cover Design: Daniel Day
Editor: Margaret Bam

For My Sons, Daniel, David and Jude

Barcelona, Spain

Spain

Spain is a **country**.

A country is land that is controlled by a **single government**. Countries are also called **nations, states, or nation-states**.

Countries can be **different sizes**. Some countries are big and others are small.

Barcelona, Spain

Where Is Spain?

Spain is located in the continent of **Europe.**

A continent is **a massive area of land that is separated from others by water or other natural features**.

Spain is situated in the southern part of Europe.

The Cathedral of Madrid, Spain

Capital

The capital of Spain is Madrid

Madrid is located in the **central part** of the country.

Madrid is the largest city in Spain.

Mijas, Spain

Regions

Spain is a country that is made up of 17 administrative regions.

The regions of Spain are as follows:

Andalusia, Catalonia, Community of Madrid, Valencian Community, Galicia, Castile and León, Basque Country, Castilla-La Mancha, Canary Islands, Region of Murcia, Aragon, Extremadura, Balearic Islands, Asturias, Navarre, Cantabria and La Rioja.

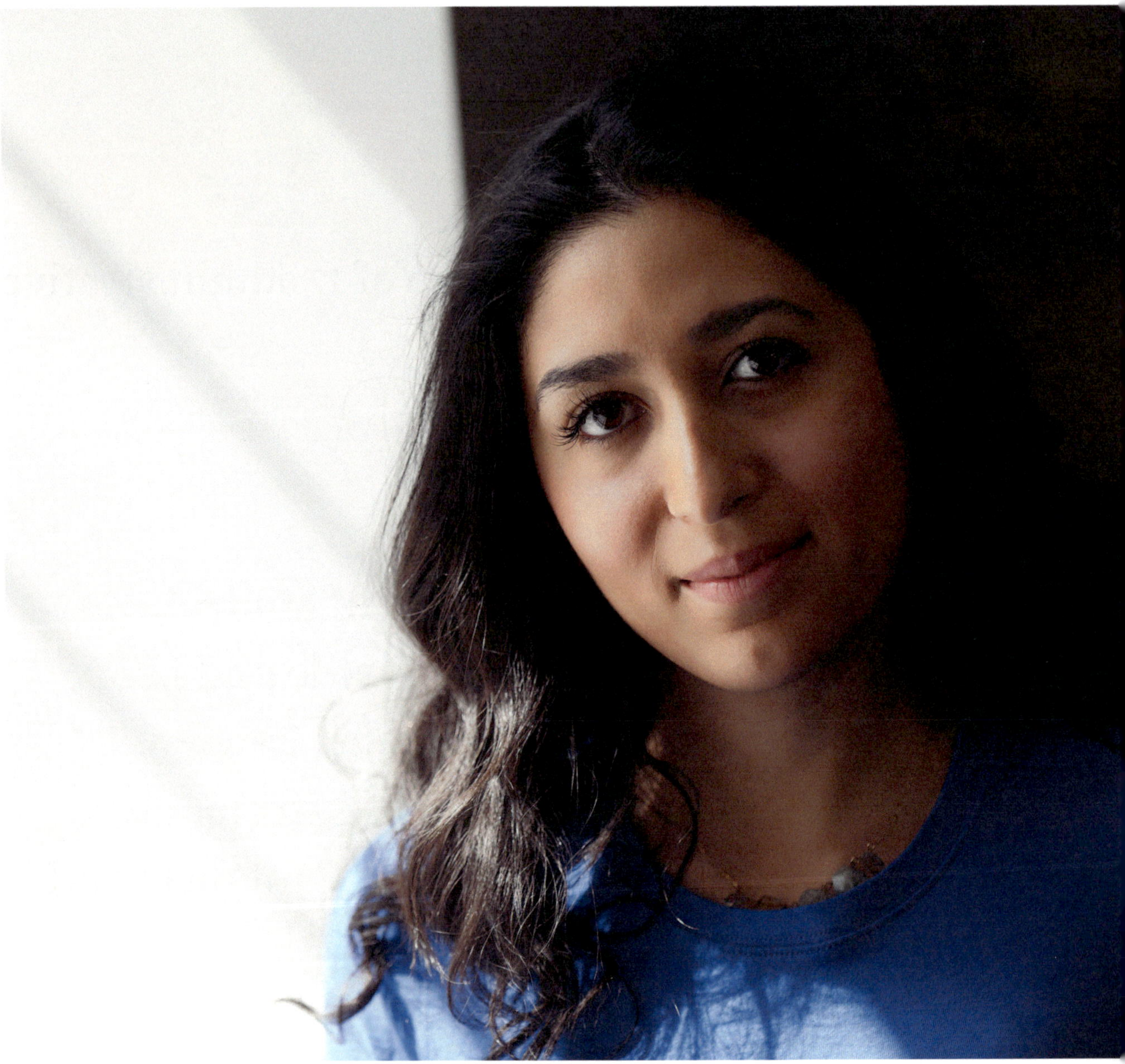

Population

Spain has population of around **47 million people** making it the 31st most populated country in the world and the sixth most populated country in Europe.

Madrid is the most populated city in Spain, with a population of over 3 million people. Barcelona, Valencia, and Seville are also large cities with populations over 800,000.

Old Town, Calp, Spain

Size

Spain is **505,990 square kilometres** making it the fourth largest country in Europe and the 51st largest country in the world.

Spain shares borders with Portugal to the west and France to the north.

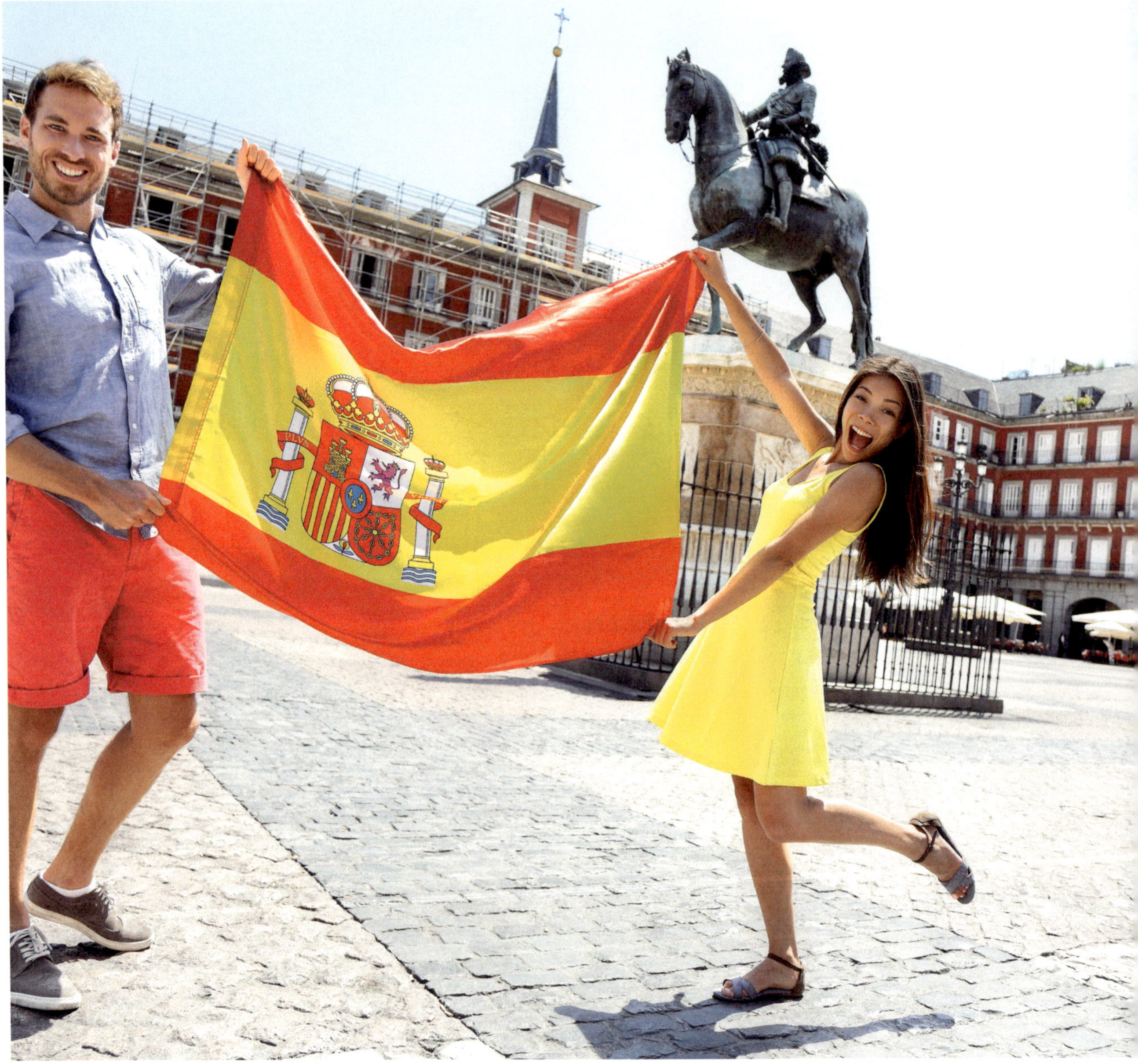

Languages

The official language of Spain is **Spanish**. The Spanish language originated in Spain and is now spoken by hundreds of millions of people across the world.

Spain is the world's fourth most spoken language.

Here are a few Spanish phrases
- **Bienvenido** - Welcome
- **¿Cómo te llamas?** - What is your name?

Parc Guell, Barcelona, Spain

Attractions

There are lots of interesting places to see in Spain.

Some beautiful places to visit in Spain are

- La Sagrada Familia
- Park Güell
- Alhambra
- Museo Nacional del Prado
- Ciudad de las Artes y las Ciencias
- Royal Palace of Madrid

Ibiza, Spain

History of Spain

Spain has a long and rich history, with evidence of human habitation dating back to the Paleolithic era. Spain was later ruled by the Roman Empire, the Moors, and the Habsburg and Bourbon dynasties.

The Spanish Empire was not only one of the first global empires, it was among the largest empires in world history. In the 16th century, Spain and Portugal began an European global exploration and colonial expansion.

Bullfighting

Customs in Spain

Spain has many fascinating customs and traditions.

- Festivals are very popular in Spain. Every town or village has a local fiesta, of which locals eat, drink and have fun.
- While bullfighting has decreased in popularity over the years, the sport still plays a part in Spain's self image.
- Many Spaniards still take a daily siestas during the hottest part of the day.

Spanish dancer

Music of Spain

Music is an important part of Spanish culture, with a rich history and a variety of styles. Popular music genres in Spain include **Salsa, Merengue, Bachata, Flamenco, Cumbia and Vallenato.**

Some notable Spanish musicians include

- **Alejandro Sanz - A Spanish musician, singer and composer who won 22 Latin Grammy Awards and four Grammy Awards.**
- **Enrique Iglesias - A Spanish singer and songwriter who started his recording career in the mid-1990s.**

Seafood Paella

Food of Spain

Spain is known for having delicious, flavoursome and rich dishes.

The national dish of Spain is **Paella** which is a hearty, flavoured rice dish with vegetables and seafood.

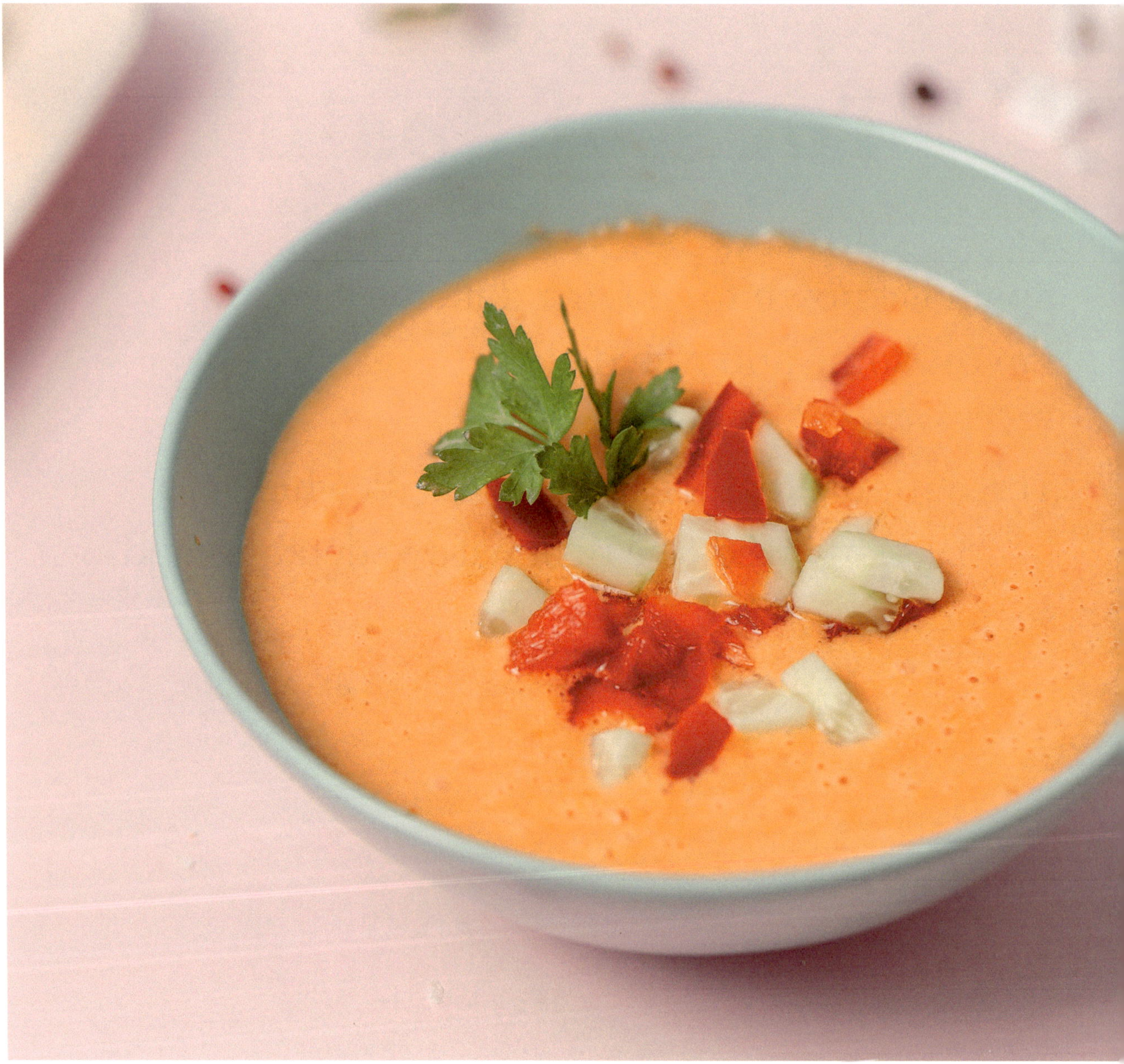

Food of Spain

Spanish cuisine is known for its diverse flavours, fresh ingredients, and regional variations.

Some popular dishes in Spain include

- **Tortilla española: A traditional Spanish omelet made with potatoes, onions, and eggs, often served as a tapa or light meal.**
- **Gazpacho: A chilled tomato-based soup made with vegetables like cucumbers, bell peppers, and garlic, often served as a refreshing summer dish.**

Seville Plaza de Espana, Andalucía

Weather in Spain

Spain has a diverse climate due to its geography and location. The northern part of the country has a temperate climate with more rain and cooler temperatures, while the south has a Mediterranean climate with hot, dry summers and mild winters.

The central region of Spain has a continental climate, with hot summers and cold winters. In some parts of the country, such as the Sierra Nevada mountain range in southern Spain, it is possible to ski in the winter.

Cat in Spain

Animals of Spain

There are many wonderful animals in Spain.

Here are some animals that live in Spain

- Boar
- Rodents
- Bears
- Bats
- Eagles
- Cats

Spanish football fans

Sports of Spain

Sports play an integral part in Spanish culture. The most popular sport is **Football.**

Here are some of famous sportspeople from Spain

- **Fernando Alonso - Formula 1**
- **Miguel Induráin - Cyclist**
- **Rafael Nadal - Tennis**
- **Raúl - Football**
- **Andrés Iniesta - Football**
- **Pau Gasol - Basketball**

Isabella II, Queen of Spain

Famous

Many successful people hail from Spain.

Here are some notable Spanish figures

- **Antonio Banderas – Actor**
- **Fernando Torres – Football Manager**
- **Pablo Picasso – Painter**
- **Queen Isabella II - Former Monarch**
- **Penélope Cruz – Actress**
- **Salvador Dalí – Painter**
- **Miguel de Cervantes - Writer**

Plaza de España, Barcelona, Catalunya, Spain

Something Extra...

As a little something extra, we are going to share some lesser known facts about Spain.

- **The Spanish national anthem contains no words.**
- **Spain is the only country in Europe that has a desert, the Tabernas Desert, which is located in the southeast of the country.**
- **Spain hosts the world's largest tomato throwing fight**

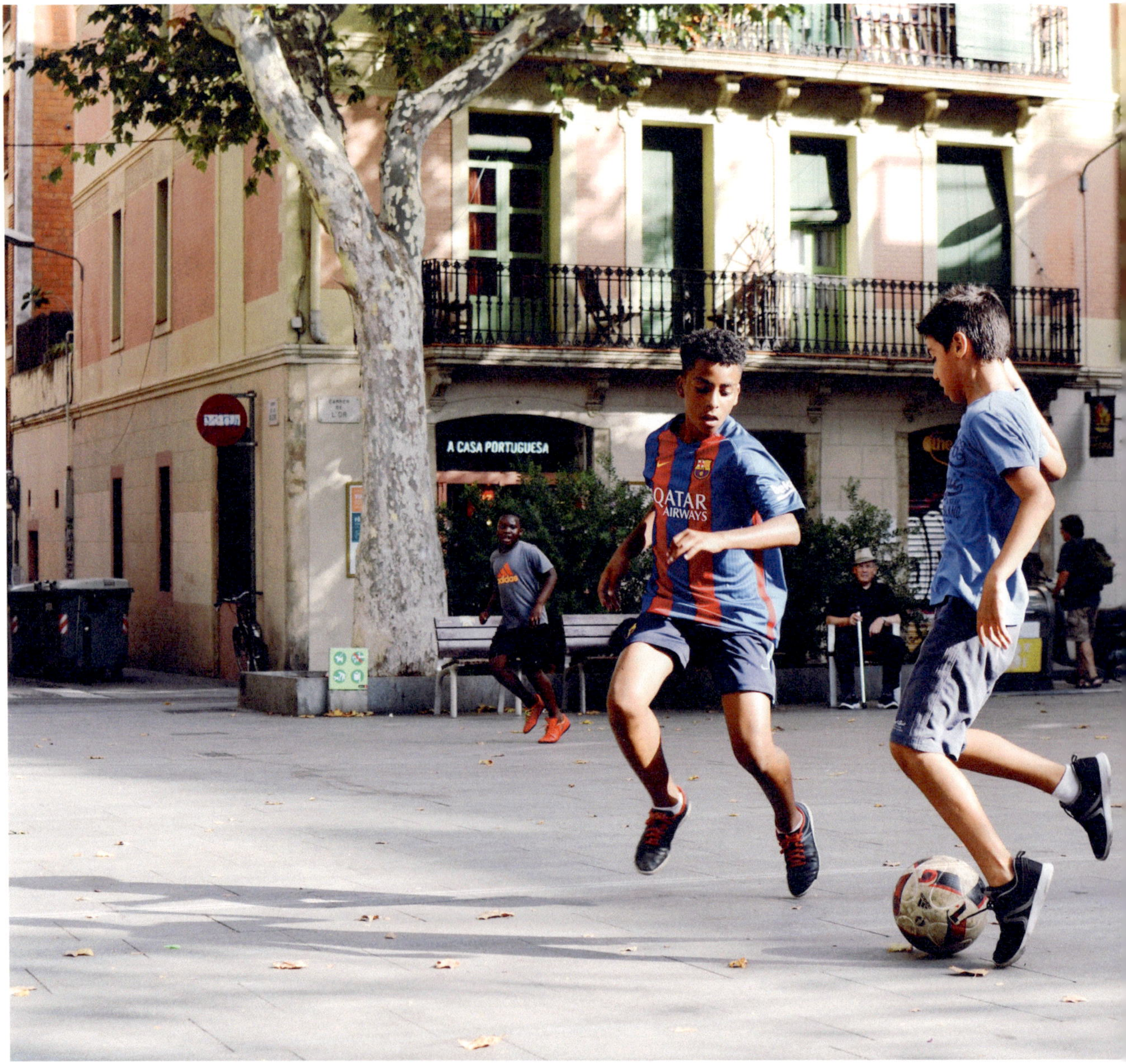
A CASA PORTUGUESA
QATAR AIRWAYS

Words From the Author

We hope that you enjoyed learning about the wonderful country of Spain.

Spain is a country rich in culture and beauty, with lots of wonderful places to visit and people to meet.

We hope you continue to learn more about this wonderful nation. If you enjoyed this book, consider leaving a review!

With Love